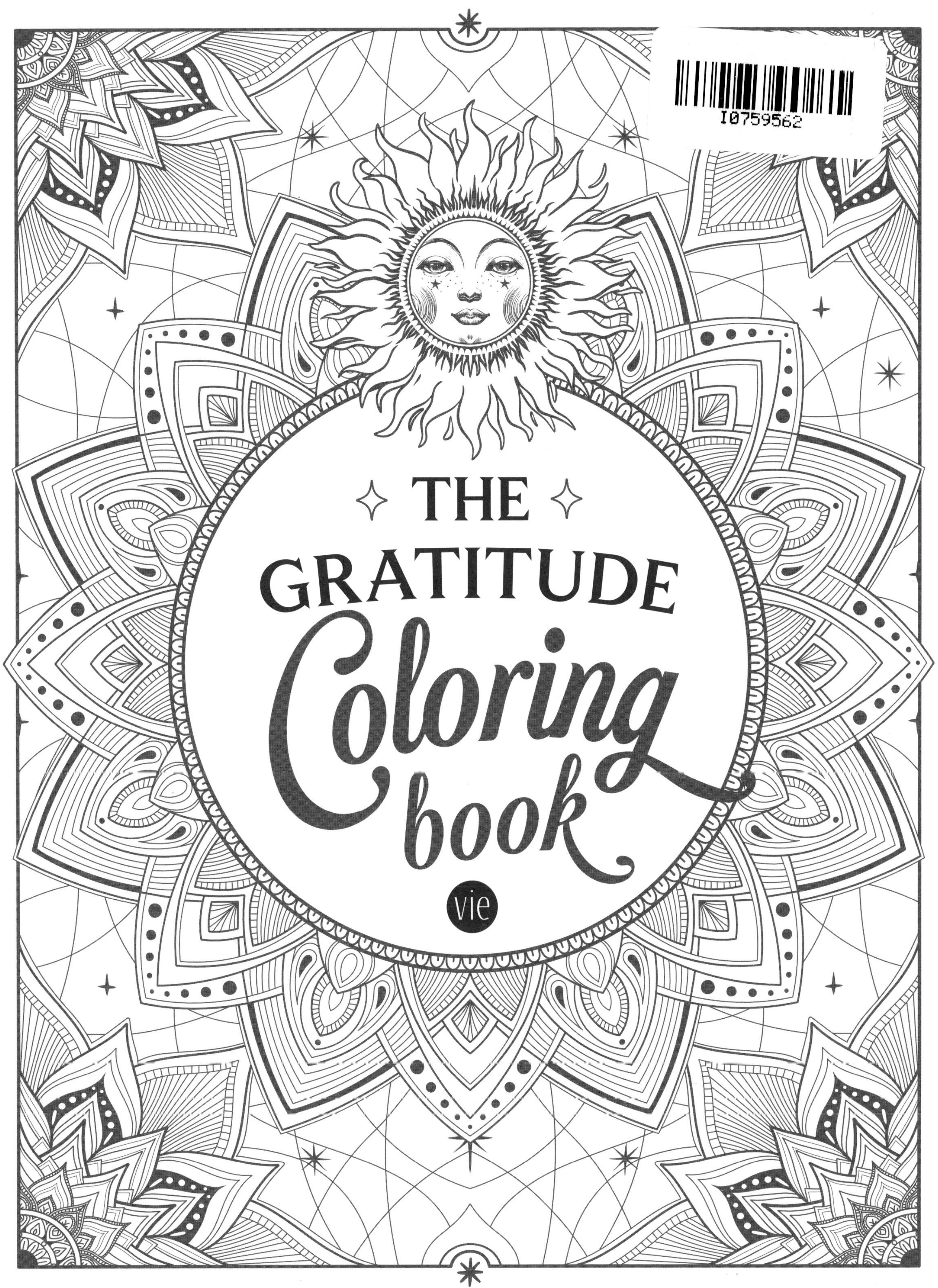
THE
GRATITUDE
Coloring
book
vie

THE GRATITUDE COLORING BOOK

Text by Siobhan Coleman and Alicia Kanik

An Hachette UK Company
www.hachette.co.uk

Vie Books, an imprint of Summersdale Publishers
Part of Octopus Publishing Group Limited
Carmelite House
50 Victoria Embankment
LONDON
EC4Y 0DZ
UK

www.summersdale.com

This FSC® label means that materials used for the product have been responsibly sourced

The authorized representative in the EEA is Hachette Ireland, 8 Castlecourt Centre, Dublin 15, D15 XTP3, Ireland (email: info@hbgi.ie)

Printed and bound in China

ISBN: 978-1-83799-618-6

To...
From..

INTRODUCTION

When life becomes busy and stressful, it can be easy to take things for granted. Our minds get clogged up with thoughts of work troubles and day-to-day demands, leaving us no time to pause and appreciate the little things. This is why gratitude is so important – and don't just take our word for it; science says so too. Studies have shown that regularly expressing gratitude can decrease depression, anxiety and the risk of illness, and improve mood, sleep and immunity. So, when it comes to starting your own gratitude practice, there really is no time like the present.

But what is gratitude and how can we practice it? Gratitude involves showing appreciation for the things in life that are meaningful and valuable to you. You don't have to live a lavish lifestyle in order to feel grateful, nor do you need to develop an elaborate self-care routine. Gratitude can be as simple as taking a few moments a day to reflect on everything you're thankful for – even small things, such as the air in your lungs, the feel of a breeze or the sound of birdsong.

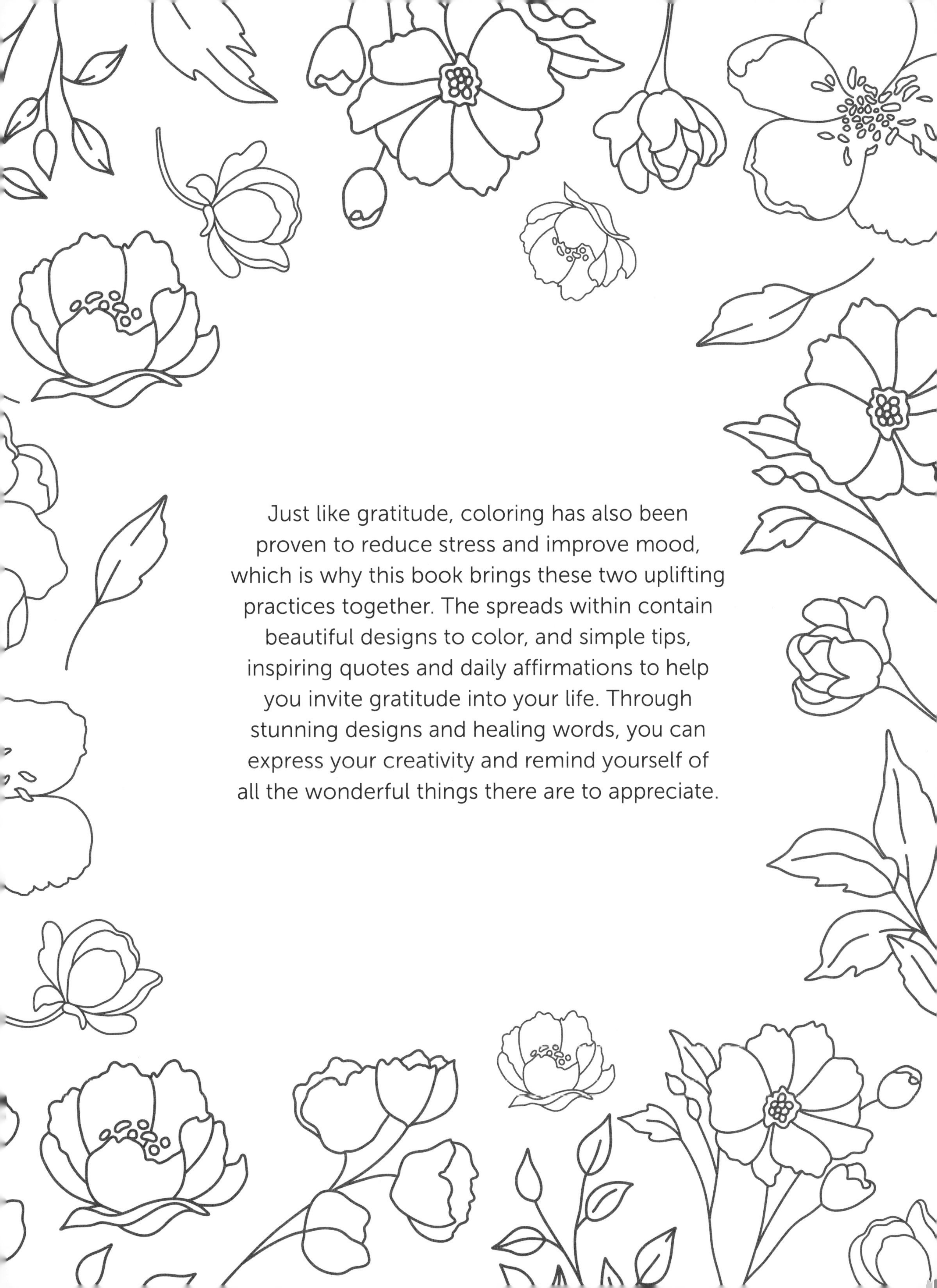

Just like gratitude, coloring has also been proven to reduce stress and improve mood, which is why this book brings these two uplifting practices together. The spreads within contain beautiful designs to color, and simple tips, inspiring quotes and daily affirmations to help you invite gratitude into your life. Through stunning designs and healing words, you can express your creativity and remind yourself of all the wonderful things there are to appreciate.

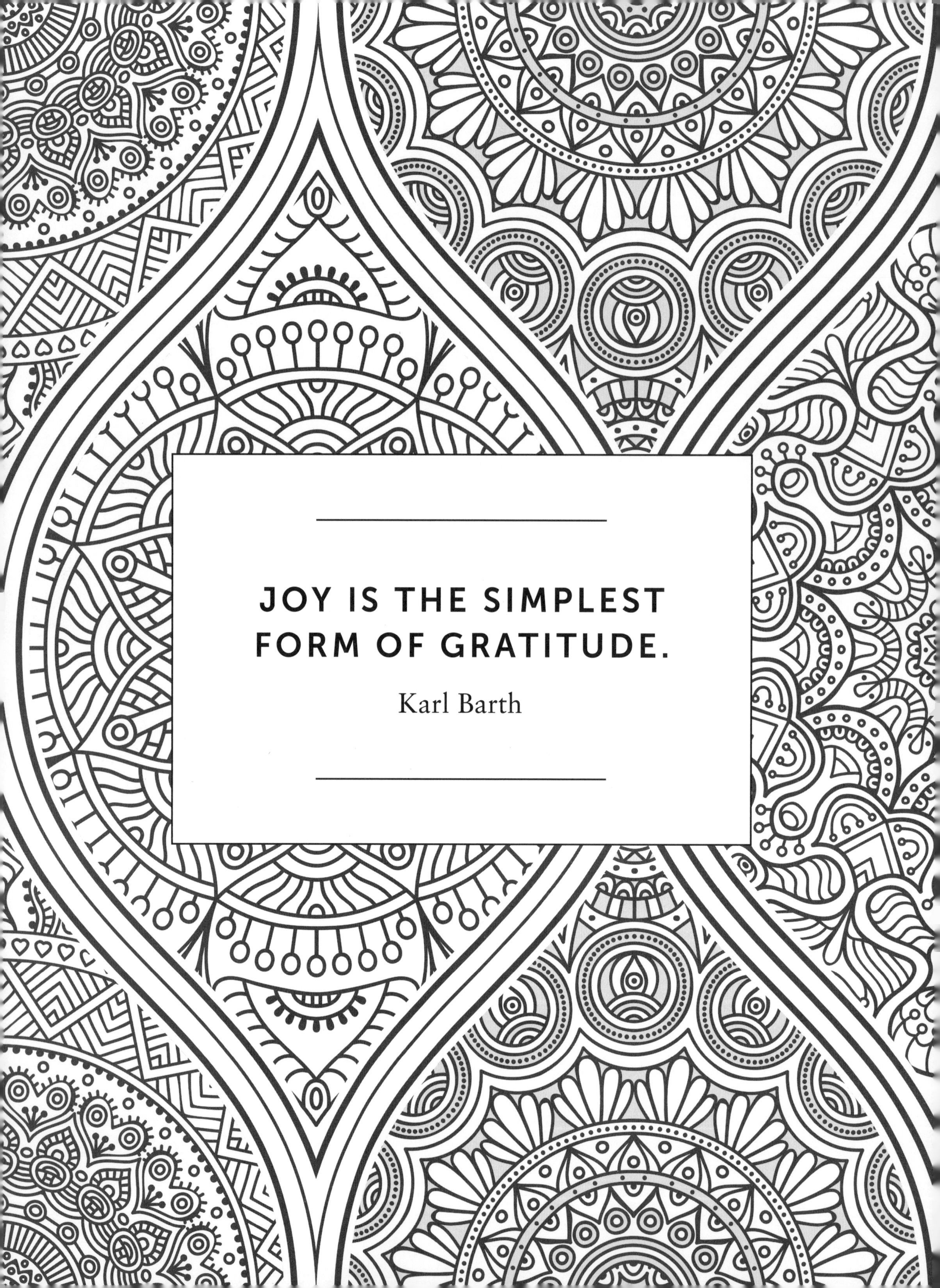
JOY IS THE SIMPLEST
FORM OF GRATITUDE.
Karl Barth

OBSERVE THE WORLD AROUND YOU

There are wonderful things happening all the time, all around us, right before our very eyes. Take a moment right now to absorb your surroundings. Whether you're in your living room, on a train, in the park or anywhere else, pause for a moment and look around. Can you see anything that you are grateful for? If you're outdoors, it might be that you feel thankful for the sunshine on your face or the smell of freshly cut grass. If you're indoors, it might be the warmth of your blanket or the company of a friend or partner. Wherever you are, whatever the time, there is always something to be grateful for.

I am
grateful
for my
life

"Thank you" expresses extreme gratitude, humility, understanding.
Alice Walker

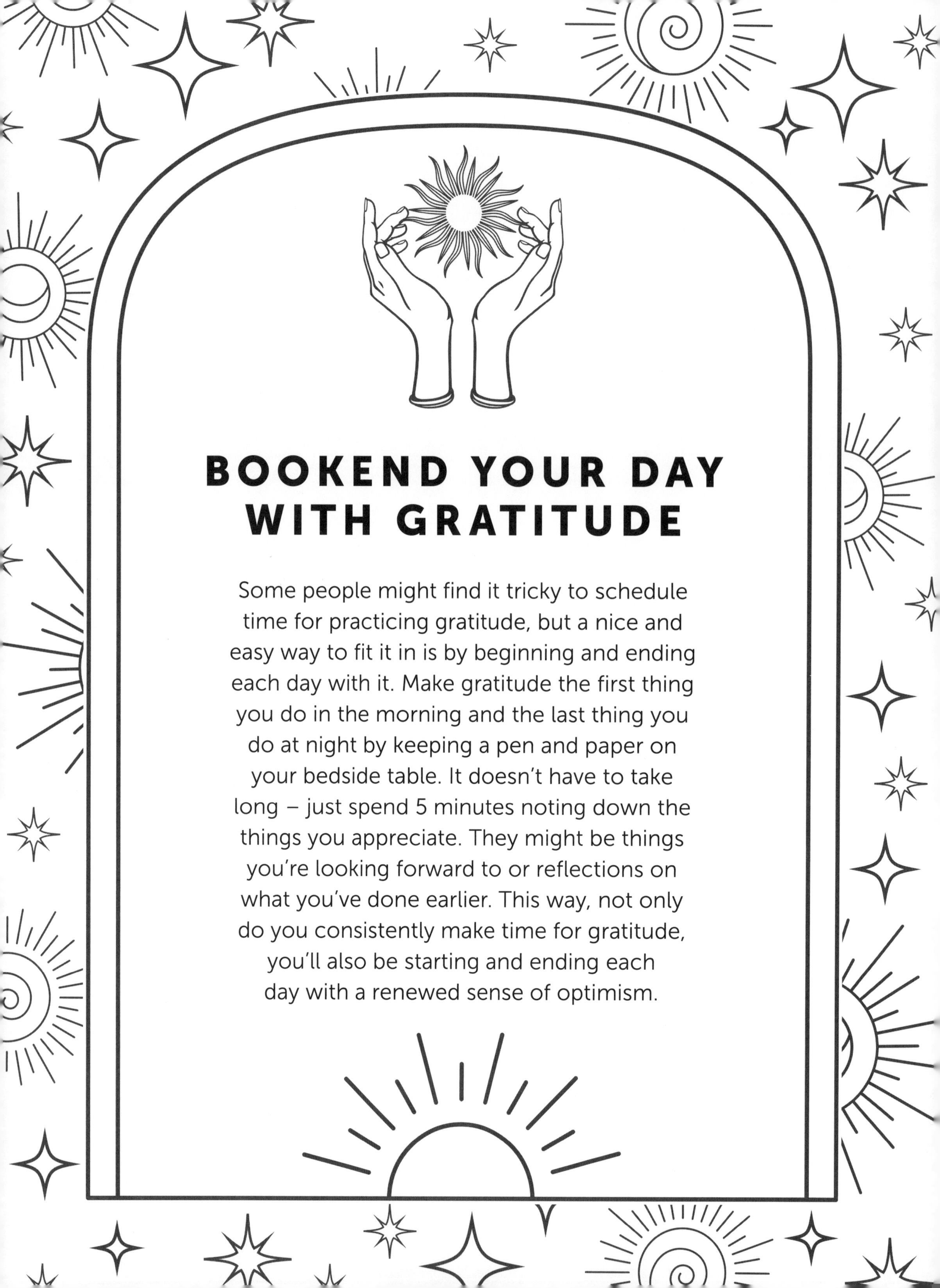

BOOKEND YOUR DAY WITH GRATITUDE

Some people might find it tricky to schedule time for practicing gratitude, but a nice and easy way to fit it in is by beginning and ending each day with it. Make gratitude the first thing you do in the morning and the last thing you do at night by keeping a pen and paper on your bedside table. It doesn't have to take long – just spend 5 minutes noting down the things you appreciate. They might be things you're looking forward to or reflections on what you've done earlier. This way, not only do you consistently make time for gratitude, you'll also be starting and ending each day with a renewed sense of optimism.

Today, I
have an
attitude of
gratitude

BE PRESENT IN ALL
THINGS AND THANKFUL
FOR ALL THINGS.
Maya Angelou

SHOW GRATITUDE FOR OTHERS

When it comes to the things we're grateful for, what probably tops the list for most of us is our loved ones. But we don't always make our appreciation for them known.

Studies have shown that expressing love can have many health benefits, for you and the person on the receiving end, including lower stress hormones, lower cholesterol and a stronger immune system. It can also help strengthen your relationship and solidify your bond.

Next time you see your best friend, partner or close family member, make a conscious effort to tell them how much they mean to you. For instance, you could say: "I am really grateful to have you in my life." It'll make their day and fill you with gratitude.

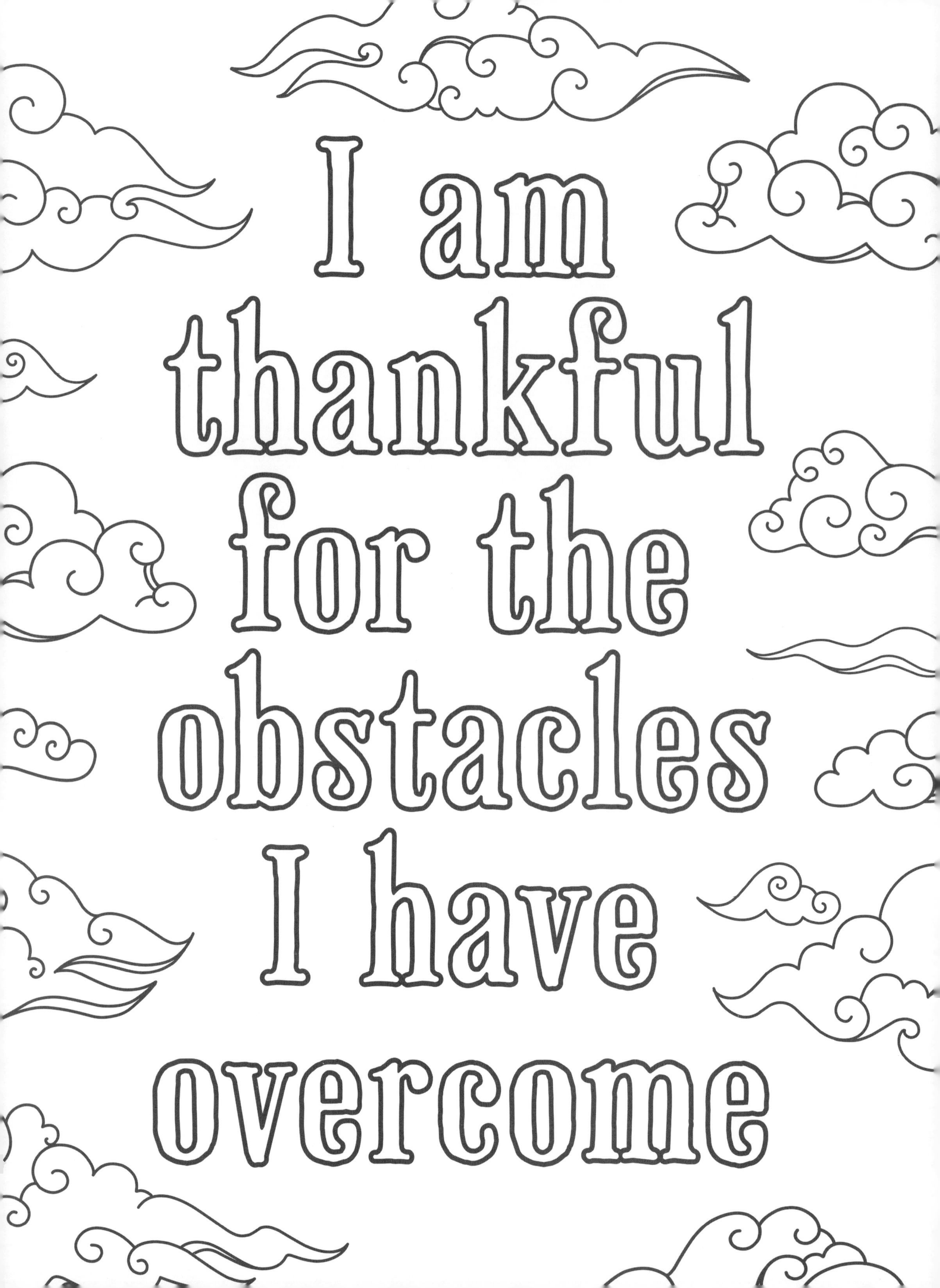
I am
thankful
for the
obstacles
I have
overcome

We can complain because rose bushes have thorns, or rejoice because thorns have roses.
Alphonse Karr

APPRECIATE YOUR SENSES

We experience the world through our senses – the ability to touch, see, smell, taste and hear. A great way to practice gratitude is by tuning in to these senses and paying attention to the joy they bring.

Take a moment to think about the sensory experiences you are grateful for, noting them down if it helps. Perhaps you enjoy the feel of a soft pillow, the smell of flowers, the sound of running water, the taste of your favorite food or the view from your bedroom window. By appreciating your senses, you remind yourself what a gift it is to be alive.

I cherish
the
simple joys

A GRATEFUL MIND IS
A GREAT MIND WHICH
EVENTUALLY ATTRACTS
TO ITSELF GREAT THINGS.
Plato

KEEP A GRATITUDE JOURNAL

The act of journaling – keeping a written record of personal thoughts and feelings – has been widely acknowledged to have many mental health benefits, including reducing anxiety, improving self-awareness, breaking away from obsessive thinking and regulating emotions. It can also be a great tool when it comes to boosting feelings of gratitude.

There are no fixed rules about keeping a gratitude journal, and you can choose to do it in whichever way suits you. You might find it easiest to write in a stream-of-consciousness style about your day, or to make a bullet list of everything you're grateful for. Whatever you choose, writing in a gratitude journal on a regular basis can be a great way to remind yourself of all the wonderful things you have in your life.

I am
grateful
for
simply
existing

If everything
was perfect, you
would never learn
and you would
never grow.
Beyoncé

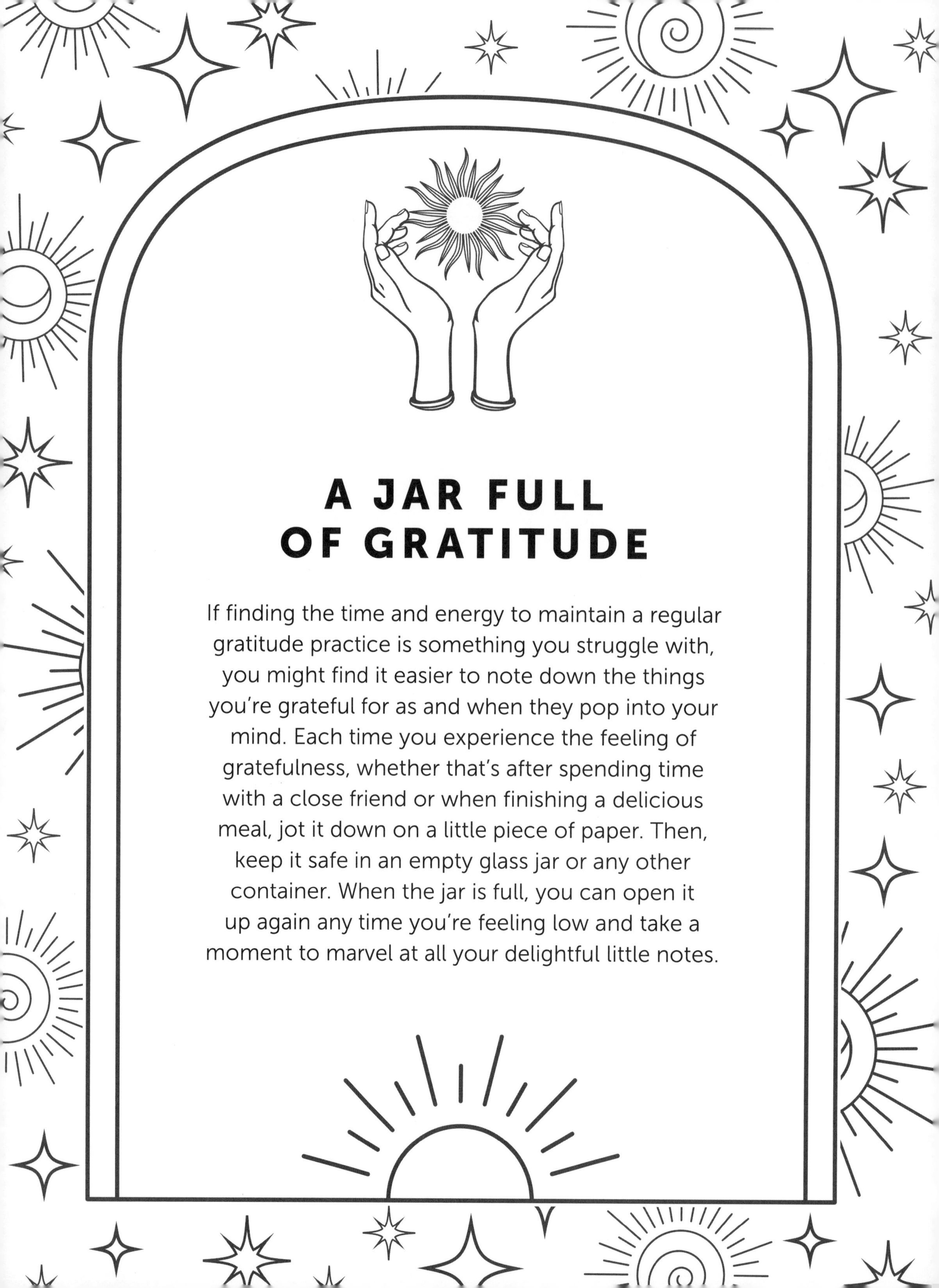

A JAR FULL OF GRATITUDE

If finding the time and energy to maintain a regular gratitude practice is something you struggle with, you might find it easier to note down the things you're grateful for as and when they pop into your mind. Each time you experience the feeling of gratefulness, whether that's after spending time with a close friend or when finishing a delicious meal, jot it down on a little piece of paper. Then, keep it safe in an empty glass jar or any other container. When the jar is full, you can open it up again any time you're feeling low and take a moment to marvel at all your delightful little notes.

My
life is
full of
blessings

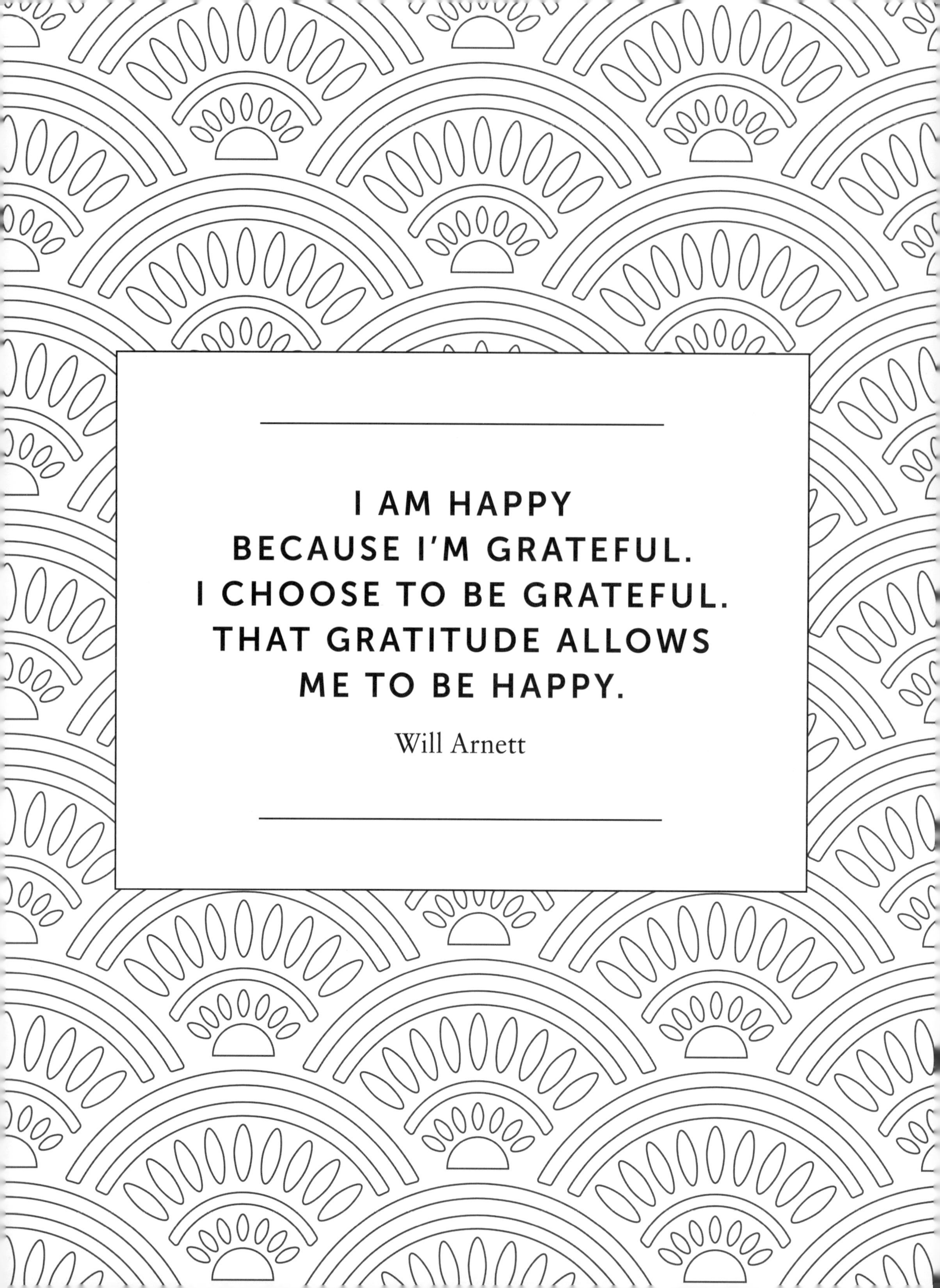

I AM HAPPY
BECAUSE I'M GRATEFUL.
I CHOOSE TO BE GRATEFUL.
THAT GRATITUDE ALLOWS
ME TO BE HAPPY.

Will Arnett

GIVE SOMETHING BACK

Feeling grateful isn't just about benefiting yourself; helping others can also foster a deep sense of gratitude. By volunteering your time, donating to a cause that means a lot to you or performing a random act of kindness for a stranger, you will experience the sense of fulfillment that comes from giving. Volunteering for a charitable cause can also expose you to a range of perspectives and challenges that can renew gratitude for your own life and the privileges you might take for granted. What's more, witnessing the impact you have on others will help you appreciate the amazing skills and talents that you possess and all you have to offer the world.

Gratitude
fills my
soul

Rest and
be thankful.
William Wordsworth

A GRATEFUL WALK

Sometimes it can be difficult to experience gratitude, particularly when you're not in the right frame of mind. No matter how hard things can seem, one irrefutable truth always remains the same: the world is a beautiful place and there are many incredible things in it to appreciate.

A great way to restore a sense of gratitude is by taking a walk in nature. By admiring the natural beauty all around you, you can fully appreciate just how lucky we are to live on this gorgeous planet. Whatever struggles you are facing, there is nothing quite like the sight of a sunset or the sound of wind rushing through the trees to remind you that there is still so much to celebrate.

I am
thankful
for my
friends
and family

GRATITUDE IS THE BEGINNING OF WISDOM. STATED DIFFERENTLY, TRUE WISDOM CANNOT BE OBTAINED UNLESS IT IS BUILT ON A FOUNDATION OF TRUE HUMILITY AND GRATITUDE.

Gordon B. Hinckley

VISUALIZE YOUR GRATITUDE

Our brains all work differently – some of us find it easiest to process our thoughts through words and written notes, while others are more visual. If you identify more with the latter, then you might find that creating a visual representation of your gratitude is the best practice for you.

Try taking photos everywhere you go – perhaps using an instant print camera – so that you can create a collage of all the things you're grateful for. You could also try sticking mementos to your collage, like concert tickets or boarding passes from a favorite holiday. Every time you look at your collage, you'll instantly be transported to those incredible moments once again.

I invite
gratitude
into my
heart

Gratitude
makes everything
that we have more
than enough.
Susan L. Taylor

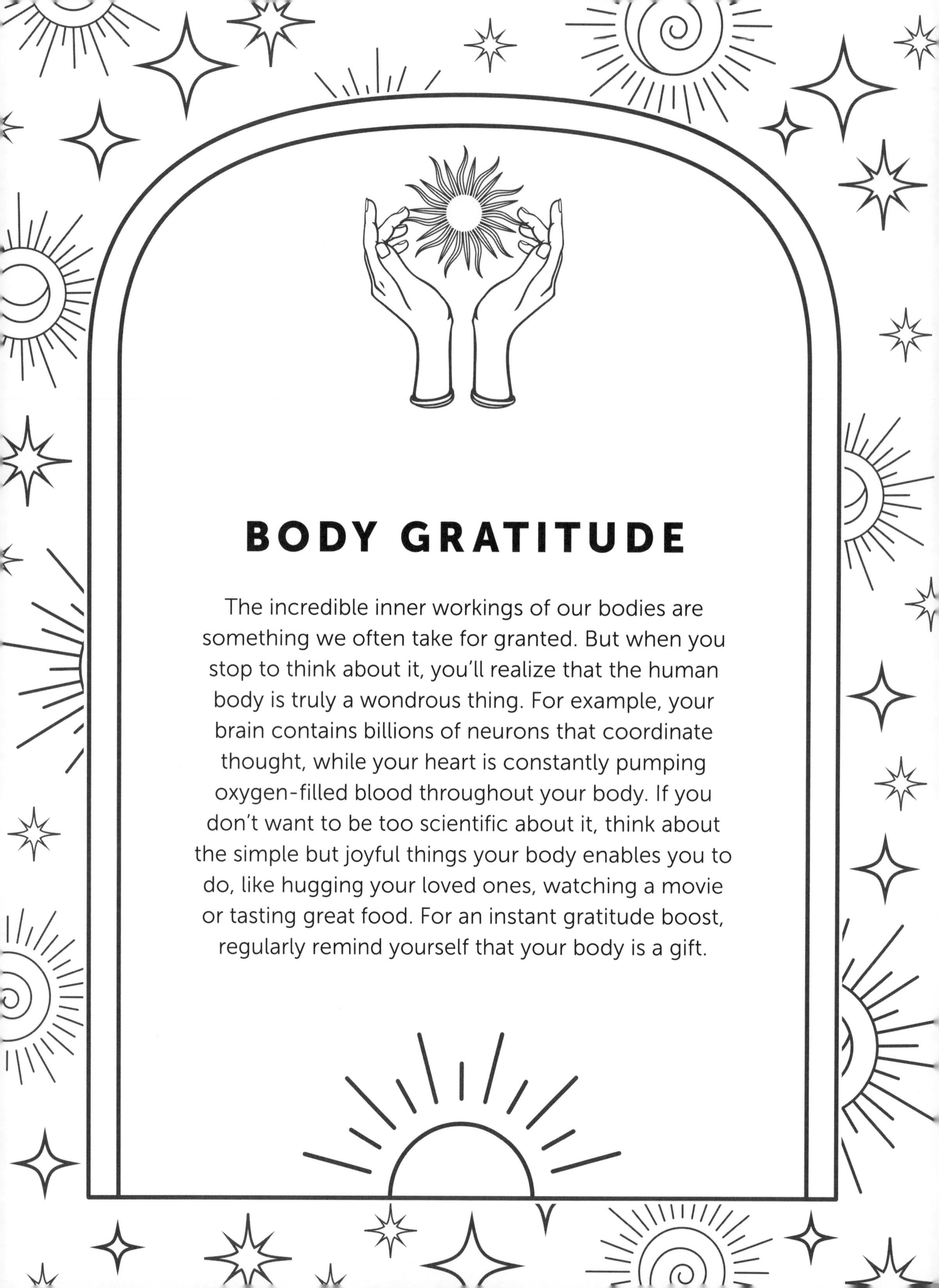

BODY GRATITUDE

The incredible inner workings of our bodies are something we often take for granted. But when you stop to think about it, you'll realize that the human body is truly a wondrous thing. For example, your brain contains billions of neurons that coordinate thought, while your heart is constantly pumping oxygen-filled blood throughout your body. If you don't want to be too scientific about it, think about the simple but joyful things your body enables you to do, like hugging your loved ones, watching a movie or tasting great food. For an instant gratitude boost, regularly remind yourself that your body is a gift.

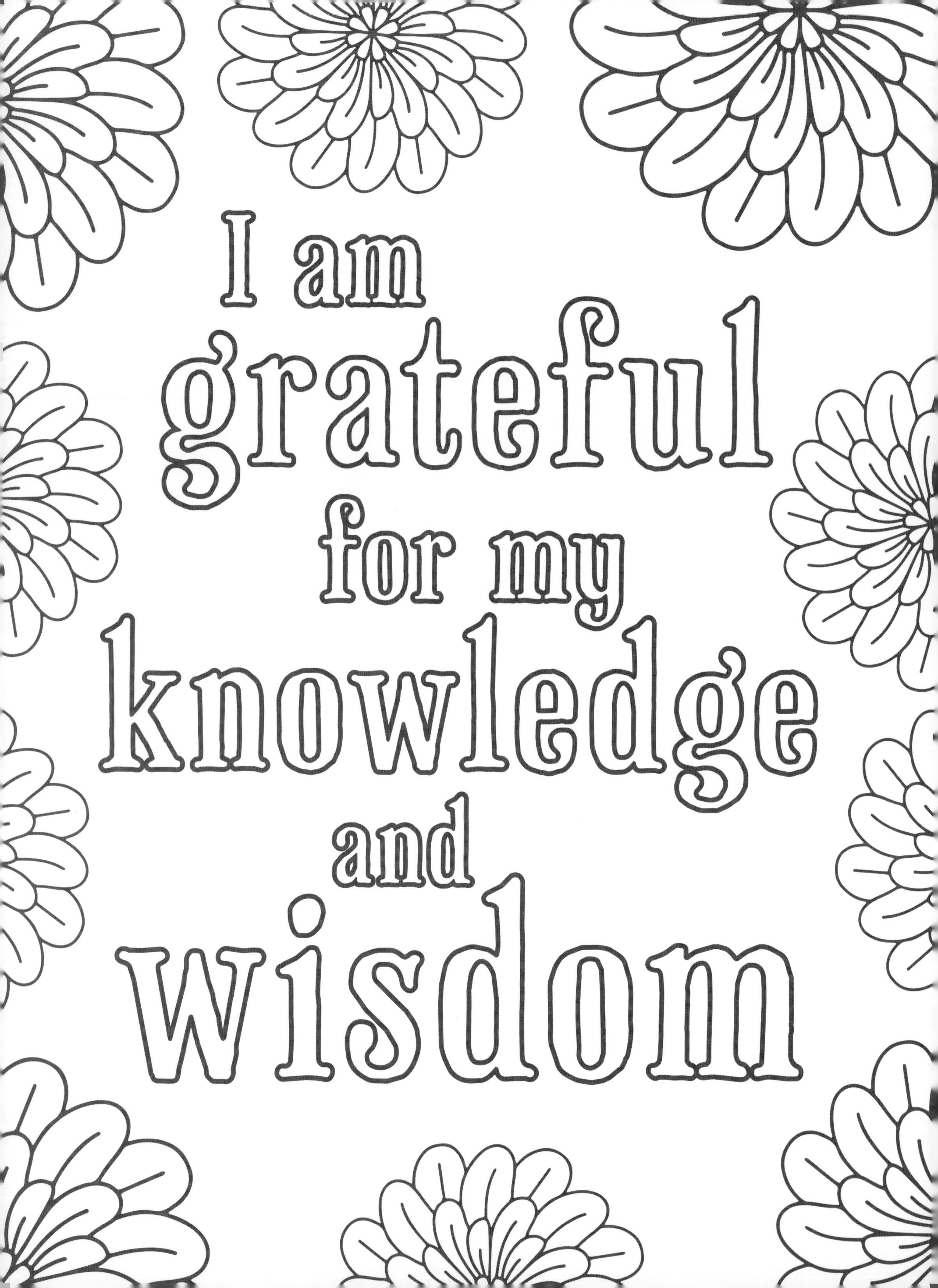
I am
grateful
for my
knowledge
and
wisdom

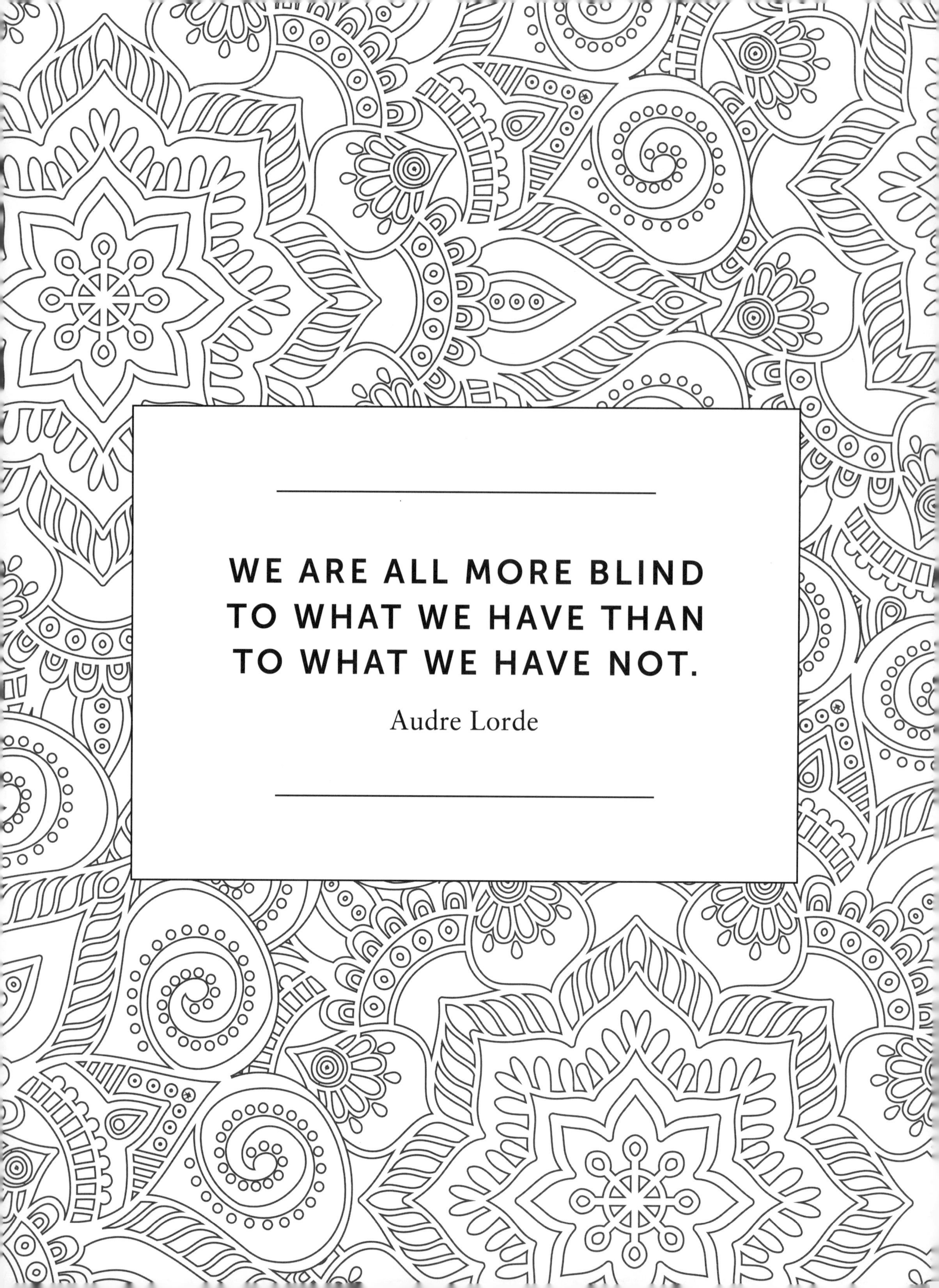
WE ARE ALL MORE BLIND
TO WHAT WE HAVE THAN
TO WHAT WE HAVE NOT.
Audre Lorde

REFRAMING PAST EVENTS

When you experience setbacks and disappointments, it can be tempting to try to completely erase them from your memory. But by reframing them instead, you can discover a new-found appreciation for all your life experiences.

Whatever the setback – whether it was the time you failed an exam, had an argument with a friend or went through a break-up – ask yourself: "How did it contribute to my growth?" and "What lessons did I learn?" This will help you to see the experience in a more positive light and feel grateful for how far you have come.

Abundance
flows
to
me

Gratitude helps you
to grow and expand;
gratitude brings joy and
laughter into your life
and into the lives of all
those around you.
Eileen Caddy

SAY "THANK YOU"

So many people work hard to help us every day: friends and family, but also shopkeepers, bus drivers, waiting staff and sometimes even random strangers. Whenever someone helps you, it's important to thank them – not just out of common courtesy, but because it makes them feel appreciated and fosters a more positive interaction. What's more, making a conscious effort to say "Thank you" is a great way to remind yourself of how much there is to be grateful for. Every time you say it, you will be filled with appreciation for all the goodness that exists in the world.

I am grateful for my ability to love

AS WE EXPRESS OUR
GRATITUDE, WE MUST
NEVER FORGET THAT
THE HIGHEST APPRECIATION
IS NOT TO UTTER WORDS,
BUT TO LIVE BY THEM.
John F. Kennedy

FOCUS ON YOUR STRENGTHS

We've said it before and we'll say it again: there are so many things to be grateful for. But perhaps most important of all is the gratitude we have for ourselves.

Of course, as humans, we tend to focus on the things we don't like about ourselves, which is why it's so important to redirect our attention to the positives. Focus on your strengths and write them down if it helps you. Ask yourself "What am I good at?" and "What can I do that no one else can?" It might be a particular hobby that you excel at, such as painting, or an aspect of your personality you really like, such as your sense of humor. By regularly reminding yourself of your greatest strengths, you will foster deeper gratitude for the person in the mirror.

I treasure every experience

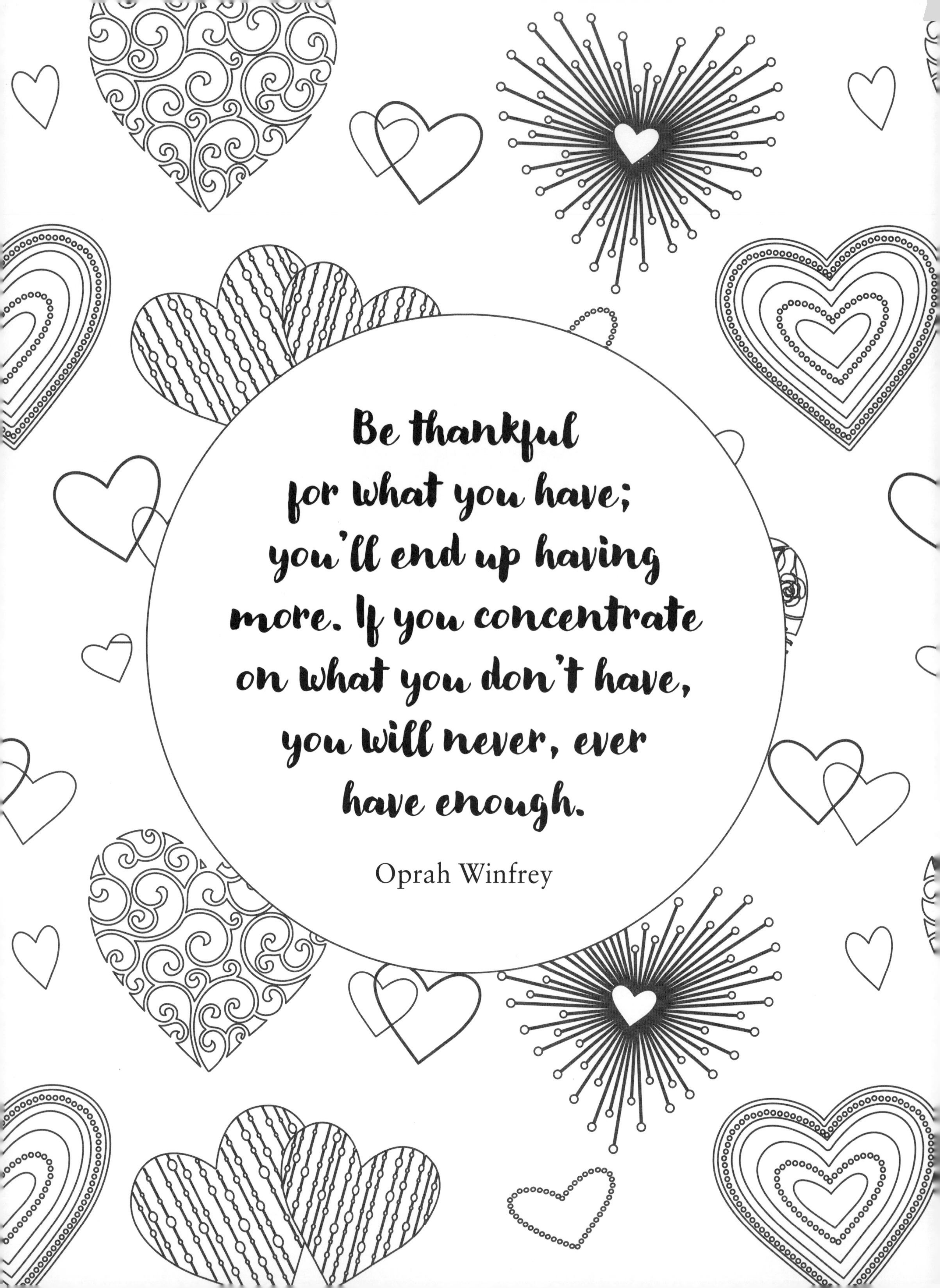
Be thankful
for what you have;
you'll end up having
more. If you concentrate
on what you don't have,
you will never, ever
have enough.
Oprah Winfrey

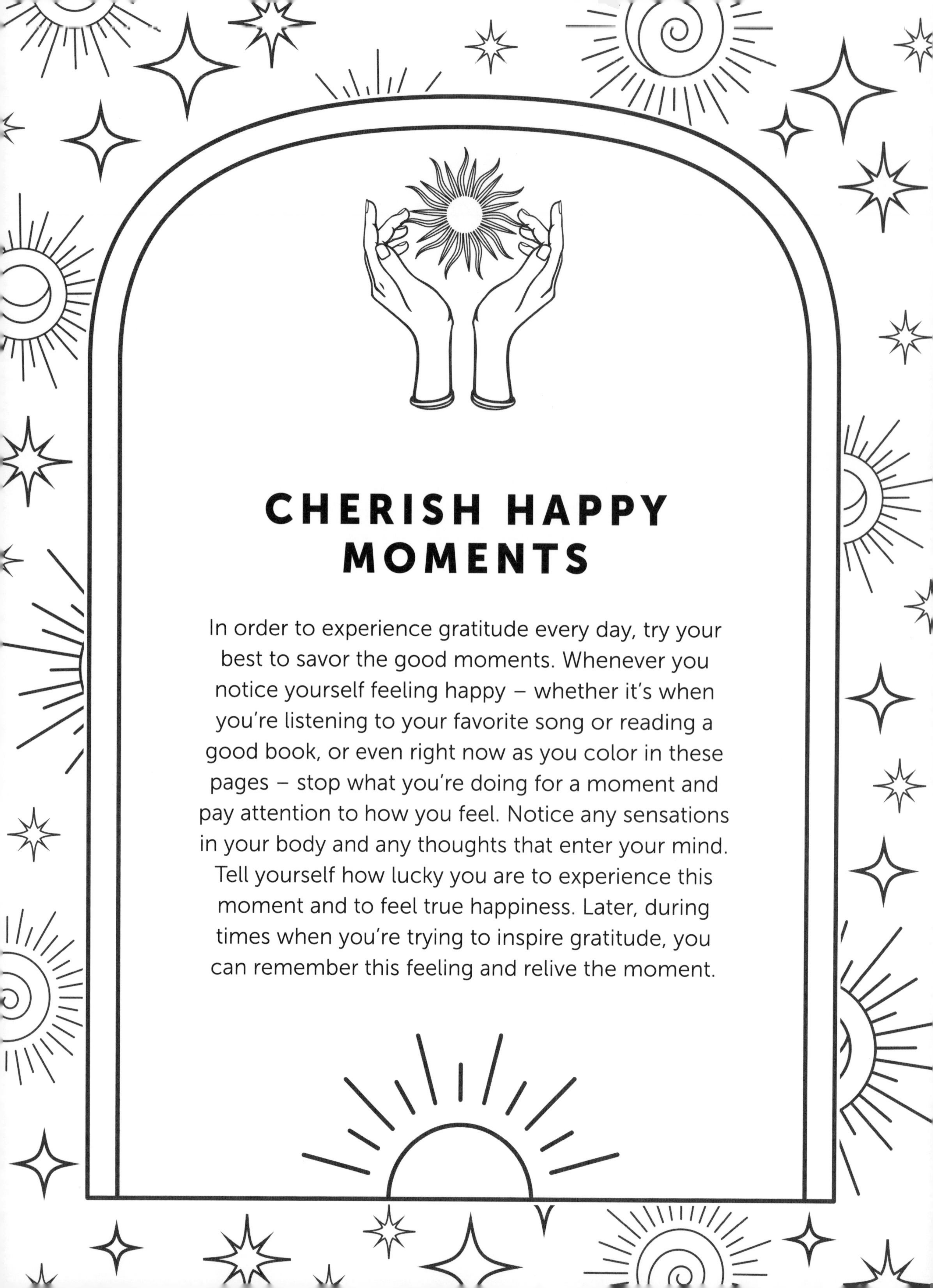

CHERISH HAPPY MOMENTS

In order to experience gratitude every day, try your best to savor the good moments. Whenever you notice yourself feeling happy – whether it's when you're listening to your favorite song or reading a good book, or even right now as you color in these pages – stop what you're doing for a moment and pay attention to how you feel. Notice any sensations in your body and any thoughts that enter your mind. Tell yourself how lucky you are to experience this moment and to feel true happiness. Later, during times when you're trying to inspire gratitude, you can remember this feeling and relive the moment.

I am grateful for my adventures

I DOVE INTO THE OCEAN
OF GRATITUDE AND NEVER
FOUND THE SHORE.
Patch Adams

I am grateful for being me

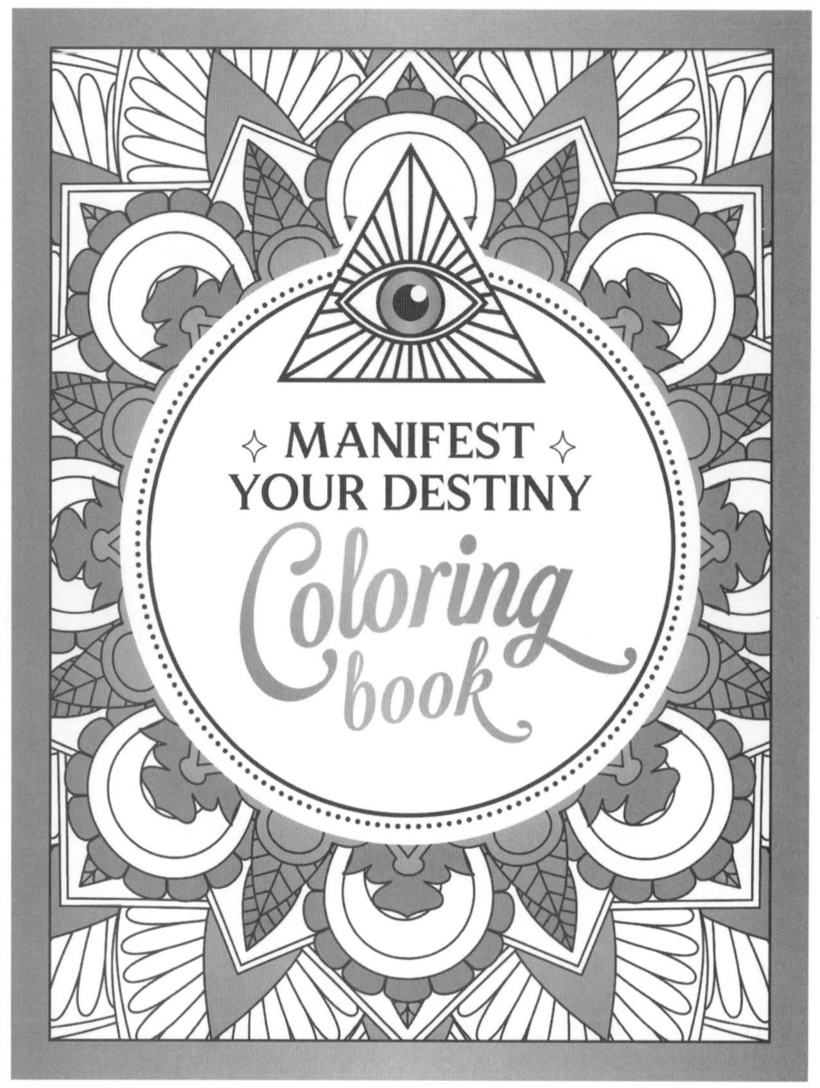

MANIFEST YOUR DESTINY COLORING BOOK

A Mesmerizing Journey of Color and Creativity

Paperback

ISBN: 978-1-83799-100-6

Discover the secret to manifesting your dreams with these pages, full of enchanting images and helpful guidance. These intricate patterns will help boost your creativity, raise your vibrations and ultimately support you on your manifesting journey. So relax, and let the universe guide you.

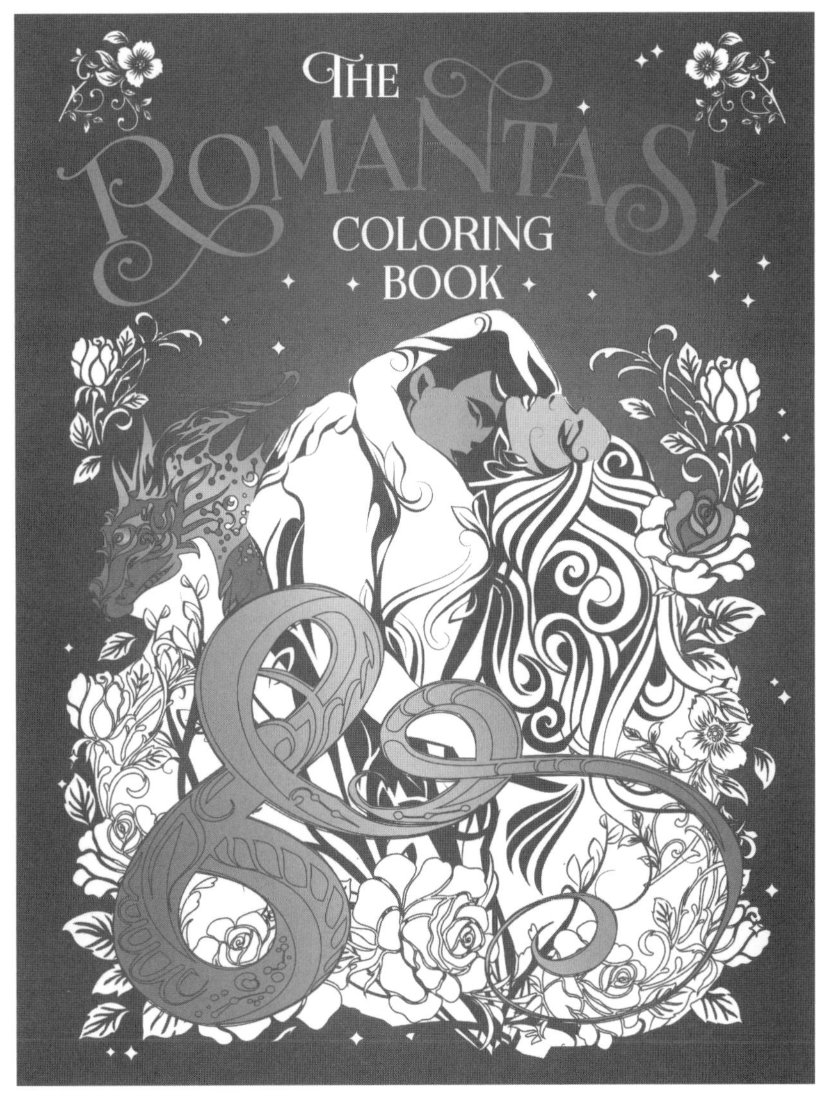

THE ROMANTASY COLORING BOOK

A Fantastical Journey of Color and Creativity

Paperback

ISBN: 978-1-83799-606-3

Step into the world of romantasy and bring this stunning collection of images to life with color. *The Romantasy Coloring Book* provides the perfect opportunity for you to unleash your passion for romance and fantasy as you embark on your own artistic adventure.

Have you enjoyed this book?
If so, find us on Facebook at **Summersdale Publishers**, on Twitter/X at **@Summersdale** and on Instagram and TikTok at **@summersdalebooks** and get in touch.
We'd love to hear from you!

www.summersdale.com

IMAGE CREDITS

p.3 and throughout – frame © Polina Tomtosova/Shutterstock.com; suns © Marish/Shutterstock.com; sparkles © AspctStyle/Shutterstock.com; hands © Zvereva Yana/Shutterstock.com; pp.4–5 – flowers © Feodora_21; pp.6–7 – mandala pattern © ViSnezh/Shutterstock.com; p.9 – mountain landscape © gurjigur/Shutterstock.com; p.10 – flowers © maritel/Shutterstock.com; p.11 – floral pattern © photo-nuke/Shutterstock.com; pp.12–13 – wave pattern © Kim Natalka/Shutterstock.com; p.15 – books and butterflies © MD_Saim/Shutterstock.com; p.16 – sun icons © Mooikunst/Shutterstock.com; p.17 – sun rise © SomjaiKing/Shutterstock.com; pp.18–19 – butterflies © VudiArts/Shutterstock.com; p.21 – heart mandala © jsabirova/Shutterstock.com; p.22 – clouds © SpicyTruffel/Shutterstock.com; p.23 – moon and stars © Verock/Shutterstock.com; pp.24–25 – flowers © Katia Karpei/Shutterstock.com; p.27 – window view © MD_Saim/Shutterstock.com; p.28 – hot air balloons © Mia Shaly/Shutterstock.com; p.29 – hot air balloons and clouds © Verock/Shutterstock.com; pp.30–31 – abstract pattern © OlichO/Shutterstock.com; p.33 – hat scene © Vlasenko Katy/Shutterstock.com; p.34 – Earth © Mateusz Atroszko/Shutterstock.com; dark Earth © juart99/Shutterstock.com; p.35 – planets © Elena Ipatova/Shutterstock.com; sparkles © AspctStyle/Shutterstock.com; pp.36–37 – flower pattern © Sweet Citrus/Shutterstock.com; flowers and leaves © Feodora_21/Shutterstock.com; p.39 – flower jar © gurjigur/Shutterstock.com; p.40 – crown © bewalruss/Shutterstock.com; p.41 – winged heart © gurjigur/Shutterstock.com; pp.42–43 – sunshine pattern © Pannawish/Shutterstock.com; p.45 – bouquet © MD_Saim/Shutterstock.com; p.46 – leaves © MG Drachal/Shutterstock.com; p.47 – leaf pattern © photo-nuke/Shutterstock.com; pp.48–49 – stars, suns and moons © Random Illustrator/Shutterstock.com; esoteric symbols © Arina Gladyisheva/Shutterstock.com; p.51 – nature garden © MD_Saim/Shutterstock.com; p.52 – patterned hearts © Anna Pogulyaeva/Shutterstock.com; p.53 – heart strings © Alka5051/Shutterstock.com; pp.54–55 – books and quills © Trixy Gatto/Shutterstock.com; p.57 – camera © Vlasenko Katy/Shutterstock.com; p.58 – butterflies © ONYXprj/Shutterstock.com; p.59 – butterfly and flowers © Lexver/Shutterstock.com; butterflies © ONYXprj/Shutterstock.com; pp.60–61 – floral pattern © IrinaKrivoruchko/Shutterstock.com; p.63 – smoothie bowl © Vlasenko Katy/Shutterstock.com; p.64 – flower head © legdrubma/Shutterstock.com; p.65 – all-seeing eye © Kulik Oksana/Shutterstock.com; eye of providence © Gorbash Varvara/Shutterstock.com; flower head © legdrubma/Shutterstock.com; pp.66–67 – petal pattern © ViSnezh/Shutterstock.com; p.69 – hourglass © nialowwa/Shutterstock.com; p.70 – waves © dhtgip/Shutterstock.com; p.71 – waves and palm trees © Davor Ratkovic/Shutterstock.com; pp.72–73 – botanical pattern © Marylia/Shutterstock.com; p.75 – tea scene © TanyaBanku/Shutterstock.com; p.76 – bouquets © Vodoleyka/Shutterstock.com; p.77 – flowers © Levitskaya Inna/Shutterstock.com; pp.78–79 – swirl pattern © Marina Sun/Shutterstock.com; p.81 – bridge scene © MD_Saim/Shutterstock.com; p.82 – sparkles © AspctStyle/Shutterstock.com; p.83 – star strings © Verock/Shutterstock.com; pp.84–85 – hearts background © Olly Molly/Shutterstock.com; p.87 – beach scene © MD_Saim/Shutterstock.com; p.88 – trees © ivector/Shutterstock.com; p.89 – mountain scene © Vlasenko Katy/Shutterstock.com; pp.90–91 – shells © Arios Elisabeth/Shutterstock.com; p.92 – hand and heart © Merfin/Shutterstock.com; p.93 – patterned heart © Watercolor_bird/Shutterstock.com